The History of Medicine

Medicine in the Industrial World

John D. Clare

ENCHANTED LION BOOKS
New York

First American Edition published in 2006 by
Enchanted Lion Books
45 Main Street, Suite 519
Brooklyn, NY 11201

Commissioning editor: Victoria Brooker
Editor: Hayley Leach
Inside design: Peta Morey
Cover design: Hodder Wayland
Consultant: Dr Robert Arnott, University of Birmingham Medical School

A CIP record is on file with the Library of Congress

ISBN 1-59270-039-X

Printed and bound in China

Picture Acknowledgements. The author and Publisher would like to thank the
following for allowing their pictures to be reproduced in this publication:
The Advertising Archives 53; AFP/Getty Images 24; akg-images 8; Archives
Charmet/Bridgeman Art Library 15 and title page; The Art Archive/British
Museum/Eileen Tweedy 38; The Art Archive/Tate Gallery London/Eileen Tweedy 56;
John Bavosi/Science PhotoLibrary 43; Chris Beetles, London, U.K./Bridgeman Art
Library 47; Bettmann/Corbis 8, 17, 25, 29, 32, 34, 35, 40 and cover, 49, 55 and
index page, 57, 58; Bibliotheque des Arts Decoratifs, Paris, France, Archives
Charmet/Bridgeman Art Library 59; Stanley B. Burns, MD and the Burns Archive
NY/Science Photo Library 41; © Burstein Collection/Corbis 54; Patrice
Cartier/Bridgeman Art Library 39; Jean-Loup Charmet/Science Photo Library 7, 14;
Corbis 19, 36, 37; Getty Images 5, 19; Historical Picture Archive/Corbis 48
(bottom); Hulton-Deutsch Collection/Corbis 33; Mary Evans Picture Library 23;
New-York Historical Society, New York, USA/Bridgeman Art Library 51; Roger
Ressmeyer/Corbis 16; Science Photo Library 21, 26, 42, 48 (top); Barbara
Singer/Bridgeman Art Library 45; Time Life Pictures/Getty Images 52; Wellcome
Library, London 4, 6, 10, 11 and 60, 12, 13, 20, 22, 28, 30, 27, 44, 46

Contents

Chapter 1
The world of 1800-1914   4

Chapter 2
How did knowledge about the body improve?   10

Chapter 3
How did knowledge about disease increase?   18

Chapter 4
How did public health improve?   30

Chapter 5
What were the advances in surgery?   38

Chapter 6
How did treatment improve?   44

Chapter 7
How successful was nineteenth century medicine?   56

Glossary   60
Timeline   62
Further information   63
Index   64

Chapter 1

The world of 1800-1914

Creating a problem

The nineteenth century saw the coming of the Industrial Revolution—particularly in Britain, France, Germany and America—and the changes it brought altered the face of medicine forever.

Working in the new factories and mines led to a whole range of occupational diseases—such as cancers, poisoning, lung diseases and dermatitis— as well as new, horrific machine injuries. The rapidly-growing cities swamped existing systems for dealing with refuse and sewage, and caused "filth" diseases such as typhus (a disease passed on by lice), tuberculosis and cholera. Acute infectious diseases such as whooping cough and scarlet fever swept through populations crowded together in the urban slums. At the same time there were increases in social diseases such as alcoholism and syphilis, and the American psychiatrist Amariah Brigham (1798–1849) attributed the growth of mental breakdowns and "nervous diseases" to the stress and hectic pace of industrial life.

Traders and empire-builders travelled to different parts of the world encountering a range of new diseases—for instance yellow fever and malaria—that sometimes simply killed them outright or which they introduced to their home countries.

William Hogarth's *Consultation of Physicians* (1736) is sometimes called *The Company of Undertakers*, presumably because Hogarth was suggesting that the doctors actually killed their patients. A group of doctors study a urine flask. They sniff posies in the end of their sticks because they think this will prevent them from catching a disease.

The eighteenth century doctor

Facing these new diseases was a medical profession utterly inadequate to the task. In 1800, although some doctors were influential members of society and friends of the rich and powerful, most struggled to make a living and had to supplement their income by farming or land deals. In the United States, after the American Revolution, there were so few doctors that clergymen often doubled up as physicians.

Eighteenth century doctors made house calls on the wealthy, with all the tools of their profession in a single bag. Relationships were personal and—although they knew about anatomy and could recognize a range of diseases—their chief function was to reassure. They had a number of medicaments and drugs to alleviate the symptoms of the illnesses they commonly encountered, but they were largely powerless to cure disease. Some of their treatments were so unpleasant and harmful that the American poet and doctor Oliver Wendell Holmes (1809–1894) suggested that if all medicines were sunk to the bottom of the ocean "it would be all the better for mankind—and all the worse for the fishes."

The doctors caricatured by Hogarth were not typical of all doctors, many of whom were important and well-respected men. The famous American doctor Benjamin Rush (1745–1813)— sometimes called the "father of American medicine"— was one of the men who signed the American Declaration of Independence, and in 1797 he was appointed Treasurer of the United States Mint.

Heroes of health?

Historians have taken two approaches to the study of the history of medicine. Until recently, medical historians tended to emphasize the scientific developments of medicine, and their accounts viewed medical progress as the result of advances made by remarkable individuals—the so-called "heroes of health." More recently, however, historians have chosen to stress the wider underlying social and economic developments. This is called the social history of medicine.

The cholera epidemic of 1831-1832

In 1817, a virulent form of cholera broke out in Jessore, near Calcutta in India. From there it passed to Bombay (1818) and then, six years later, it spread through Persia — despite the guns that villagers fired to try and frighten it away. When it reached Russia in 1830, the government used troops to try to blockade infected villages. The strategy did not work: the disease travelled into Sweden, where strict quarantine rules also failed to stop it from spreading.

Meanwhile, a ship from Cairo brought cholera to mainland Europe in 1831. Spain introduced the death penalty for bringing cholera into the country. In Hungary, mobs accused the wealthy of poisoning the wells. In Germany, beggars who claimed to be infected promised to go away if they were paid. In Paris, the first victim dropped dead during a masked ball, sparking a panic evacuation to the countryside. Cholera killed

The *Sunderland Herald* of 1831 described the symptoms of cholera as: "Vomiting or purging of a liquid like rice-water...the face becomes sharp and shrunken, the eyes sink and look wild, the lips, face, neck, hands and feet, and the whole surface of the body is leaden, blue, purple, black...The skin is deadly cold, the tongue flabby and chilled like a piece of dead flesh. The respiration is often quick but irregular...In the treatment of this disease it is necessary to state that no specific remedy has yet been discovered."

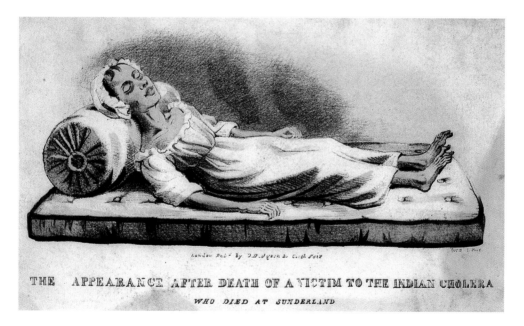

THE APPEARANCE AFTER DEATH OF A VICTIM TO THE INDIAN CHOLERA
WHO DIED AT SUNDERLAND

nearly 22,000 people in Britain alone between 1831–1833.

In 1832, a boatload of Irish immigrants took the disease to Montréal in Canada, from where it worked its way down to New York. On June 26, 1832, the first victim—an Irish immigrant named Fitzgerald—fell ill, and the disease killed 3,500 people in the next two months. This caused a general flight of inhabitants, which in turn spread the disease further through America.

Endemic diseases

Cholera made people panic. Consequently, governments began to look for ways to make advances in public health. In actuality, however, many nineteenth century diseases were more deadly than cholera. Tuberculosis was probably the biggest killer, along with childbirth, while dysentery and childhood illnesses like scarlet fever killed many children. Hookworm was common in the south and malaria in the Mid-West. Slaves, Native Americans and, later, those who migrated west were particularly vulnerable to disease, as were urban slum dwellers.

The bacillus *vibrio cholerae* (a germ transmitted in the faeces of humans) is common and normally benign. In 1996, however, US researchers discovered that the cholera toxin is carried by a virus, and when this virus infects *vibrio cholerae* the resultant strain is virulent. There were renewed pandemics in 1849 and 1866. This illustration, still showing cholera as the "grim reaper," is from a French magazine of December 1912.

King cholera

The cholera epidemic of 1831–1832 gives us an insight into how ineffective the medicine of the nineteenth century was. Cholera arrived suddenly and killed quickly and horribly. Although it afflicted primarily the poor and the weak, it killed the wealthy and the strong as well. Suggested therapies included immense dosages of laudanum (opium), rubbing the body with mustard, tobacco smoke enemas, electric shock therapy, and oilcloth plugs to try to stop the diarrhoea. Nothing worked. Cholera demonstrated the powerlessness of humankind in the face of disease in the nineteenth century.

LE CHOLÉRA

The means to a solution

Although the Industrial Revolution created many medical problems, it also stimulated great advances in technology and science. Improvements in machine tools and mechanical engineering led to new medical instruments and machines as well as railway trains and factory machinery. Improved communications, such as photographs, the telegraph and the wireless, allowed new medical knowledge to be shared and applied all over the world.

It was not just that medicine had access to new chemicals and machines—though both were to revolutionize medicine by the end of the nineteenth century. The change in attitudes and beliefs that came with the Industrial Revolution also created a culture in which medical discoveries were possible. New political theories such as democracy and socialism, which stressed the rights of all people, led ordinary people to demand access to medical care. Changing ideas about the role and abilities of women led to women doctors and a revolution in nursing. The ideas of Charles Darwin about evolution (1859) and of Gregor Mendel about genes and heredity (1869) changed what people thought about the nature of life and disease.

The front page of Darwin's *The Origin of Species* (1859). Darwin's ideas about evolution helped to change attitudes to medicine. People started to reason that if humankind was not God's special creation, perhaps doctors had a right to affect the nature of life.

ON

THE ORIGIN OF SPECIES

BY MEANS OF NATURAL SELECTION,

OR THE

PRESERVATION OF FAVOURED RACES IN THE STRUGGLE FOR LIFE.

By CHARLES DARWIN, M.A.,

FELLOW OF THE ROYAL, GEOLOGICAL, LINNÆAN, ETC., SOCIETIES;
AUTHOR OF ' JOURNAL OF RESEARCHES DURING H. M. S. BEAGLE'S VOYAGE
ROUND THE WORLD.'

LONDON:
JOHN MURRAY, ALBEMARLE STREET.
1859.
P. 375.

The right of Translation is reserved.

Eugenics

The new ideas of evolution and genes led the English explorer and scientist Francis Galton (1822–1911) to develop the theory that intelligence and certain physical and mental defects are hereditary. Although it reached its most wicked conclusion in Nazi Germany, the idea of "eugenics" (from the Greek meaning "well-born") was widely taken up in America in the nineteenth century. Richard Dugdale's study of a New York family of paupers and criminals, *The Jukes* (1875), led a number of states to try to stop these "defects" from being passed to the next generation. They made laws for the compulsory sterilization of the "feebleminded, insane, criminalistic, inebriate, diseased, blind, deaf, deformed and dependent."

Nationalism and war

Nationalism (the belief that one's own nation is superior to all others)—a powerful ideology in the nineteenth century—stimulated further medical advances. French and German researchers competed to make the more significant discoveries. War also helped medicine. The American Civil War honed the skills of many surgeons, improved nursing, stimulated the pharmaceutical industry and led to the foundation of the United States Soldiers' Home. The Army Medical department was at the forefront of medicine and the Marine Hospital Service led the way in hygiene. As nations scrambled to build up their empires, they developed medicines to combat tropical diseases, not to help the local people (who were often immune), but to help protect their soldiers from illness.

Medicine and war: an amputation in the field during the American Civil War.

Chapter 2

How did knowledge about the body improve?

A shortage of bodies

Well before the beginning of the nineteenth century, the Scottish obstetrician William Hunter (1718–1783) had established the need to learn anatomy by dissection. In America, William Shippen, who had studied under Hunter, started giving anatomy lectures around 1762. Using models and a skeleton, he began the first anatomy course in North America. In 1765, Shippen set up the Philadelphia Medical School.

Since doctors were only allowed to dissect the bodies of executed murderers, however, there was a severe shortage of bodies, and for many years this shortage was met, notably in Britain and America, by "resurrection men" (grave-robbers). Eventually, this

The most famous "resurrectionists" were the Irishmen William Burke and William Hare. Hare ran a lodging house in Edinburgh. When an old soldier died owing him money, Hare sold the body to a Dr Knox for more than the original debt. Sensing easy money, Hare and one of his lodgers, Burke, then began suffocating lodgers and selling the bodies. They were eventually caught, and Burke was hanged.

problem led to the sanctioning of more bodies for dissection. In Britain, the Anatomy Act of 1832 allowed doctors to dissect any body, providing the relatives agreed. In America, Massachusetts had passed a similar act the previous year, and other states followed. Nevertheless, grave robbing for dissection continued in some states up until 1900.

The popularization of anatomy

Many historians now think that during the nineteenth century, people in Britain and America learned to think of themselves as "anatomical beings." Doctors lectured artists on anatomy, and put on slide shows for the public. After the 1870s, anatomy became part of the school curriculum for both primary and secondary school pupils.

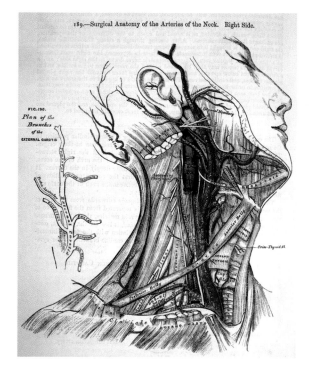

189.—Surgical Anatomy of the Arteries of the Neck. Right Side.

Applying technology

Although the microscope had been invented in the seventeenth century, it was of no use for detailed work because its single lens caused distortion and "rainbow" fringes around the edges. In 1826, Joseph Jackson Lister (father of the famous surgeon, see Chapter 5) invented a system of multiple spaced lenses which corrected the problem. This invention allowed doctors to study the cells of animals for the first time, and led to the science of histology (the study of tissues to diagnose disease).

In 1858, the Scottish anatomist Henry Gray wrote *Gray's Anatomy*, an anatomy textbook organized by systems —bones, joints, muscles, cardio-vascular systems etc. The 1918 edition had 1,247 engravings, many in color. It became hugely popular in Britain and America, and not just as a textbook for students and surgeons. In fact, many families bought their own private copy. Today it is available for free in its entirety on the Internet.

Frankenstein

Mary Shelley's novel, *Frankenstein* (first edition 1818, third edition 1831), reveals the doubts people had about anatomy at the time. In the novel, Victor Frankenstein is an anatomical surgeon, who assembles the body for his monster by robbing graves. Eventually, he is implicated in murder as a means of getting the required body parts.

The Paris school

The French Revolution changed medicine. The theory of "the rights of man," upon which the Revolution was based, included the right to health care. In 1794, the new government set up three important centers of research known as *écoles de santé* (schools of health). One of the principles of the Revolution was equality, and students of any background were admitted to these centers by open examination. At the same time, the Revolution overthrew the traditional medical authorities and allowed medical practitioners more freedom. As a result, French medicine made significant advances and the Paris hospitals became centers of medical research.

In 1816, the French doctor René Laënnec invented the stethoscope. Doctors learned to tap the patient's chest and to interpret the different sounds produced. This is called, "auscultation." Laënnec's book, *Traité de l'auscultation mediate* (*Dissertation on Indirect Auscultation*), explained in detail what doctors ought to listen for. Auscultation became the main method of internal diagnosis, and remained so until the development of X-rays.

Clinical medicine and the beginnings of physiology

One of the most influential Paris doctors was Pierre Louis. His book, *Essay on Clinical Instruction* (1834), suggested that symptoms (the outward manifestation of illness) were poor indicators of disease. What doctors should look for, he argued, were "signs," understood as changes in the processes going on *inside* the body. His ideas mark the start of clinical medicine, whereby doctors diagnosed diseases on the basis of a detailed physical examination. Indeed, having diagnosed what they thought was the disease, doctors in Paris would then dissect a patient after his death to prove that their diagnosis had been correct.

Just as important was the French doctor Francois Broussais (1772–1838), who argued that there was nothing particularly unusual about disease. There was, he said, a continuum from health to disease, and illness occurred simply when the normal functioning of the body went wrong. Doctors started to study physiology: the normal functioning of the body. Following from Broussais, the French physiologist Claude Bernard (1813–1878) studied the digestive system and developed the idea of "homeostatis"—the theory that the body is a series of systems designed to keep itself in balance, even if external conditions change. Bernard argued that physiology could only be studied in the laboratory, through animal experiments and vivisection.

One of the most influential American doctors, pictured here, was William Henry Welch (1850–1934). The ideas of the "Paris School" of doctors changed the international practice of medicine and marked the beginning of modern medicine. Students from Britain and America flocked to be taught in France and Germany. Welch studied in Germany but returned to America to run the new medical department at John Hopkins University (1884), where he insisted on European standards of scientific study and clinical laboratory work.

Experimental physiology

In 1836, the Czech physiologist Jan Purkinje – who was the first person to study brain cells under the microscope – published a memo in which he argued that physiology was a separate discipline, and that funding was needed for physiology institutes and laboratories. His ideas can be said to mark the beginning of experimental physiology, which is investigating how the body works.

Reductionism and the first physiologists

In 1847, a group of German physiologists declared the processes of the human body to be merely chemical reactions, no different from those found in the world of inorganic chemistry. This idea is known as "reductionism."

As a result, researchers began to measure and experiment on the body, and made great advances in understanding how the body works. In Germany, Hermann von Helmholtz measured the speed of electronic impulses along the nerves (1848). In Russia, Ivan Pavlov, in a famous experiment, showed that reflex responses (e.g. salivating when a dinner gong sounded) could be learned (1890s). In England, in 1902, Ernest Starling and William Bayliss discovered secretin (which stimulates the stomach to produce digestive juices), the first of many hormones to be discovered. In 1912, Casimir Funk, a Polish biochemist, discovered vitamins. After 1915, doctors identified several diseases which were caused by vitamin-deficiencies and were curable using extracts from certain foods.

In 1825, the German scientist Justus von Liebig (famous for his work on phosphate fertilizers, and as the inventor of Oxo) became Professor of Chemistry at the University of Giessen, in the German state of Hesse. Here, he encouraged his students to study the chemistry of different metabolic processes. In 1828, his co-researcher, Freidrich Wöhler, synthesized urea (pure urine), thus proving that the compounds in the human body were no different from other inorganic chemicals.

Medical machines

As part of these scientific experiments, researchers invented machines to measure the workings of the body. Carl Ludwig invented the kymograph (1847) to monitor the pulse. Wilhelm Röntgen invented X-rays (1895). And Willem Einthoven developed the electrocardiograph (c. 1900), which measured the electrical activity of the heart.

Where previously patients might have been described in general terms such as "feverish," now they were scientifically and statistically monitored. By the end of the century, doctors understood the human body as never before.

X-rays are an example of how advances in science and industry had an affect on medicine in the nineteenth century. Röntgen's first X-ray (right) was of his wife's hand, including her wedding ring. The first medical use of X-rays occurred in Liverpool in 1896, when the surgeon Robert Jones used X-rays in preparing to remove an air gun pellet from a boy's wrist.

Knowledge of the digestive system

The enthusiasm of nineteenth century doctors for physiology is well-illustrated by the following case. Alexis St. Martin was a Canadian "voyageur" (porter and canoe-man) who, in 1822, was shot at point-blank range by a shotgun. Against all expectations, Alexis recovered, but his body, in healing, left a fistula (a hole) right through into his stomach. For the rest of his life, unless this hole was plugged with wadding, half-digested food would ooze out continually.

Dr. William Beaumont, the American army surgeon who treated Alexis, was so fascinated that he took Alexis to live with him. He spent three years studying the operation of Alexis' stomach—mainly by putting food into the hole on a rope and pulling it out again later to see what had happened to it. Most doctors today are agreed that Beaumont's conduct was thoroughly unethical, but he and Alexis St. Martin substantially added to our knowledge of how the digestive system works.

Cell theory

Until the eighteenth century, doctors believed that the body was composed of four "humors," and that these four liquids (blood, phlegm, and yellow and black bile) determined the state of a person's health. Historians call this "humoral pathology."

By the start of the nineteenth century, the Paris school of doctors had begun to question this idea, suggesting that the seat of disease lay in the tissues, not in the so-called "humors." The invention of the achromatic lens by Joseph Jackson Lister (see page 11) was to destroy it altogether. In 1839, using the new microscope, the German physiologist Theodor Schwann produced his book *Mikroskopische Untersuchungen* ("Microscopic Researches") in which he showed that all animal tissues were composed of cells, not humors.

Below is a picture taken with a microscope of brain tissue full of malignant cancer cells.

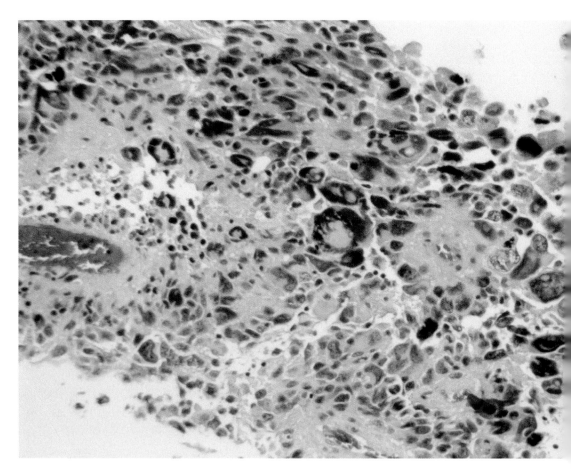

Rudolph Virchow looking through a magnifying glass. Virchow's skill in communicating his ideas is one of the reasons for his huge influence in the history of medicine.

Rudolf Virchow

Rudolf Virchow (1821–1902) was Professor of Pathological Anatomy in Berlin. He was a reductionist who believed that the body "follows the ordinary physical and chemical laws."

In 1858, Virchow published his book *Cellular Pathology* in which he proved that cells controlled all bodily events, from fertilization and growth to the formation of pus in wounds. Disease, he claimed, was the result of the abnormal development and reproduction of certain cells. This idea, he boasted correctly, marked the death of humoral pathology, and the study of disease at cell level turned out to be the foundation for the developments in curative medicine during the twentieth century.

Cancer

Virchow was especially interested in cancer. In the 1840s, he had described one of the earliest cases of leukemia and went on to make many more studies of tumors. He showed how cancer-tumors grow from cells that have mutated, but then multiply out-of-control. He suggested that cancer was caused by the body's own immune system working on areas of inflammation – an understanding which has become a key idea in the battle against cancer today.

Chapter 3

How did knowledge about disease increase?

Inoculating for smallpox

Smallpox was a terrible disease, which disfigured its victims with ugly "pockmarks" and, in its most virulent form, killed one in three people who caught it (particularly the weak, poor, old and very young).

Inoculation against smallpox was first developed by the Chinese (c. 1000 AD). Using pus from a pock of the less virulent form of the disease, and smearing it on a thread of cloth—so that the virus was greatly attenuated (weakened)—they then infected a person, perhaps by a scratch on the skin. The patient fell ill with a mild case of smallpox, but usually recovered, and was immune thereafter. This procedure was called "variolation." Lady Montagu Wortley, wife of the British Ambassador to Turkey, brought the idea of variolation back to Britain in 1721, and the American doctor James Kilpatrick introduced it in South Carolina in the year 1738.

The English doctor Robert Sutton improved the method of variolation by insisting that patients were well-rested and well-fed before they were inoculated. Nevertheless, infecting people with the live smallpox virus remained a very dangerous (and sometimes fatal) way of making people immune.

Vaccination against smallpox spread all over the world. It was made compulsory in Germany in 1835, and in Britain in 1853. In 1977, Ali Maow Maalin, a smallpox vaccinator in Somalia, contracted *variola minor* but recovered from the disease. He had the last case of smallpox in the world, and in 1980 the World Health Organization officially declared the smallpox virus extinct. There are, however, still laboratories where smallpox germs are kept alive, to be used for vaccination.

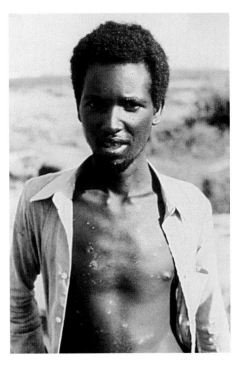

Cowpox and vaccination

Cowpox was a disease similar to smallpox, but it was not fatal. Farmers knew that people who had caught cowpox never fell ill with smallpox. In 1796, when an English girl caught cowpox, a local doctor named Edward Jenner used pus from a pock on her finger to infect a boy called James Phipps. James caught cowpox, but recovered. A month later, Jenner tried to inoculate him with smallpox, but failed—James was immune to smallpox. The American doctor Benjamin Waterhouse was impressed by Jenner's work and, in 1800, he vaccinated his son. Waterhouse helped campaign for the vaccination: he is sometimes called "the Jenner of America."

Was Jenner important in the history of medicine?

While of real practical importance, Jenner's method provided immunity from only one disease in such a way that no one understood *why* it worked until 80 years later. By using a similar disease (cowpox) and not an attenuated form of the actual disease, he provided neither clues about how to advance further, nor insight into human immunity in general. Consequently, further scientific research involving germs, germ theory and attenuation was necessary in order for doctors to understand how to fight disease. For this reason, there are those who argue that Jenner's discovery was a lucky coincidence, rather than a step in the progress of medical understanding.

The word vaccination was taken from the Latin word "vacca," meaning cow. Pasteur (see page 26) called it vaccination in honor of Jenner's work on the cowpox vaccine. Vaccination was not immediately accepted. There was a popular belief that it would turn people into cows. The Royal Society criticized Jenner, and he had to publish *An Inquiry into the Causes and Effects of the Variolae Vaccinae* (1798) at his own expense so that his ideas would become known.

What causes disease?

The Greeks taught (and doctors until the eighteenth century believed) that disease was caused by an imbalance of the humors(see page 16). During the eighteenth century, belief in the four humors died out, and doctors instead came to think that disease was caused by "miasmas" (bad smells). For example, the word "malaria" means, literally, "bad air." This idea has a basis in common sense: bad smells are closely associated both with disease and with the unsanitary conditions that cause disease. The "poisonous miasma" theory of disease persisted well into the nineteenth century and was responsible for many significant advances in public health (see Chapter 4).

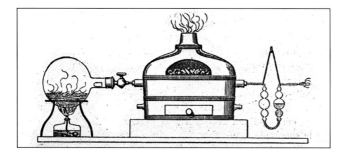

Eighteenth century doctors thought that bacteria were the result of disease, not its cause, and they developed the theory of "spontaneous generation" (the idea that the disease created the bacteria). As late as 1860, the French scientist Felix Pouchet conducted experiments, using the equipment shown, which supposedly "proved" this theory. Pouchet heated the matter to kill all existing bacteria, then he opened the jars to the air and the matter decomposed, whereupon bacteria "spontaneously" developed. However, as Pasteur proved, it was the air which carried the bacteria.

Bad smells

Most doctors in the early nineteenth century accepted the idea that foul air caused disease. French doctors compiled a "smell map" of Paris, to chart the medical geography of the city. One British workman was assured that his family had fallen ill because of his "remarkably offensive" breath and sweat! In 1855, *The Lancet* claimed that not only did smelly gases cause disease, but they also were responsible for "failing strength, flabby muscles, pallid cheeks, lassitude of body and torpidity of mind."

Doubts about miasmas

After 1800, however, an increasing number of doctors expressed doubts about the "foul air" theory of disease. They blamed "zymes" (harmful agents), which might be chemicals, fungi, parasites, or cells from another sick person's body. In 1839, the German physician Johann Schönlein discovered that the itchy skin disease

This 1866 French cartoon of death giving people water from a pump shows that people had realized that infected drinking water caused cholera. In 1854, the English doctor John Snow had proved through meticulous research that cholera cases originated from a single water source, and he stopped the epidemic by taking the handle off the pump – thus proving beyond doubt that cholera was caused, not by a miasma, but by a water-borne impurity.

ringworm was caused by a parasite and, in the 1850s, the English epidemiologist William Budd proved that typhoid was spread by an unknown agent in the faeces of people infected with the disease. Then, in 1855, the German Professor of Public Health, Max von Pettenkofer, suggested that cholera was spread by "germs," although he was unsure what "germs" actually were.

Bacteria

Scientists had known about bacteria ever since the invention of the microscope. In the late eighteenth century, a Danish scientist named Otto Müller had studied and described a number of different bacteria. In 1849, the French scientist Franz Pollender had noticed that bacteria were present in huge numbers in the blood of cattle which had died of anthrax. But doctors never imagined that these tiny, single-cell creatures could actually cause a disease that would kill a human being.

Louis Pasteur and the germ theory of disease

In the 1850s, Louis Pasteur was a French industrial chemist working on the fermentation of wines. Personal heartbreak—the death of two daughters from typhoid fever—led him to study disease. During the 1870s, Pasteur worked to establish that microbes were the cause of disease, and he isolated several disease-causing germs. It is this discovery which established him as one of the "heroes of health" (see page 5) in early medical histories. Pasteur achieved cult status, particularly in France. One encyclopaedia describes the germ theory as "probably the most important single medical discovery of all time."

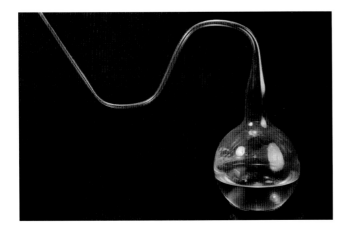

In 1864, Pasteur described the experiment in which—using a swan-necked flask—he claimed to have given the theory of spontaneous generation a "mortal blow" by *proving* that decay was caused by dust and germs falling out of the air. When he boiled milk and left it in an open flask, the milk turned sour. Boiled milk kept in a swan-necked flask—into which germs could not fall—stayed fresh.

The importance of Pasteur

Recently, however, medical historians have questioned Pasteur's importance. Today many historians believe that Pasteur did not give a single "mortal blow" to ideas about miasmas and spontaneous generation, but that they were gradually overturned over a number of years.

In fact, Pasteur was not the first to claim that "germs" caused disease, and it is arguable that the German doctor Robert Koch (see page 24-5) did more to establish that certain bacteria caused specific diseases. The germ theory in itself did not cure a single disease, and even doctors who accepted it could not really see how it was relevant to the way they treated their patients. Even in France as late as 1879, the editor of the scholarly *Concours Médical* argued that, although Pasteur's work was "a glimpse of the way ahead," it was by no means proven to be the only solution to the problem of disease: "we should maintain a certain reserve for the time being and not see bacteria everywhere, after previously seeing them nowhere."

Nevertheless, the idea that germs cause disease not only revolutionized surgery (see Chapter 6) and laid the basis for the revolutionary discovery of antibiotics in the twentieth century, it also changed forever the way people behaved. When you wash your hands after going to the toilet, you do so because you know that "germs cause disease."

Pasteurization

As part of his work on wine, Pasteur had discovered that heating the wine to 122°F killed the yeast which caused the fermentation, and stopped the wine from going sour. This process came to be called "pasteurization." Dairies in the USA and Scandinavia pioneered the practice of pasteurizing milk, thereby killing the bacteria which caused tuberculosis, typhoid, diphtheria and dysentery. Pasteurization is the process which ensures that the milk you drink is safe.

The key advances in public health and nursing (see Chapter 4) predated the germ theory, and were based on what one historian has called "the erroneous filth theory of disease" and the idea that it was morally important to be clean.

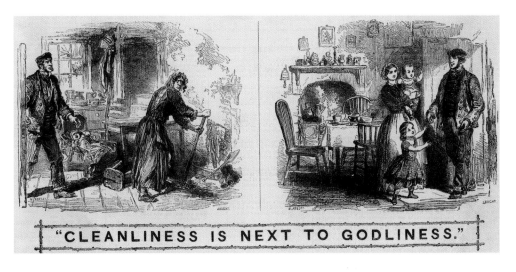

"CLEANLINESS IS NEXT TO GODLINESS."

Robert Koch and bacteriology

In 1879, Robert Koch, a District Medical Officer for
Wollstein, near Berlin, took the germ theory of disease
to its next stage. It was one step to assert that germs
cause disease. The next step was to prove that a specific
germ caused a specific disease. In 1878, Koch actually
identified the germ which caused septicaemia
in wounds. He discovered how to "stain" septicaemia
germs blue with the chemical dye methyl violet, and
how to photograph them. His assistant, Julius Petri,
discovered how to grow "cultures" of bacteria on a
substance made from potatoes and gelatine—now called
the "petri dish" and still used today by students in
their biology experiments.

Medical researchers soon
realized that one man on his
own could not do the immense
amount of work needed to
discover all the germs that
cause disease, and they began
to build up research teams.
Huge medical institutes were
set up, with government and
private funding. The first—
shown here—was the Pasteur
Institute in Paris (1888).

Koch laid down the methodology of *how* researchers
should discover the germ that caused a specific infectious
disease. Even today his rules are called, "Koch's
Postulates." They are:

1. Make sure the germ is *always* present in every case.
2. Grow a pure culture of the germ.
3. Inject the germ culture into a healthy animal to check
   that it contacts the disease.
4. The germ must be recovered from the infected animal.

The plague

In France, Pasteur and his students called themselves microbiologists; in Germany, Koch and his students called themselves "bacteriologists." There was tremendous rivalry between the two groups.

In 1894, plague broke out in Hong Kong. The first scientist to arrive there, in order to find out the cause of the disease, was a student of Koch, the Japanese researcher Shibasaburo Kitasato. He made friends with the English doctors there and set up his equipment in the local hospital. Alexandre Yersin, a student of Pasteur, arrived slightly later, carrying his microscope in one hand and his sterilizer in the other. He was forbidden to use the hospital, so he made friends with the local Catholic priest and set up a laboratory of his own.

Both men studied the blood and buboes (swellings) of infected patients and quickly discovered the culprit organism—a short stubby rod-bacterium, which was easy to stain with aniline dyes. Both men grew colonies of the bacterium on agar jelly, and both then injected it into animals to reproduce the disease. Both men then rushed their work into print. As a result of these findings, a Russian named Haffkine produced a vaccine during the Bombay epidemic in 1897. It was not very effective, however, and outbreaks of plague still occur.

Koch spent hours in his laboratory trying to identify the germs that caused particular diseases. In 1881, using a lantern and photographs, Koch showed his discoveries about the germ theory of disease to the International Medical Congress in London. Even Pasteur (who hated Germans) was forced to admit: "This is great progress, Monsieur."

Pathogens

Koch's work led to the discovery of many other pathogens (disease causing bacteria). He discovered the bacilli that cause tuberculosis (1882) and cholera (1883). In America in the 1890s, the army doctor George Sternberg discovered the bacterium that causes pneumonia, and William Welch isolated the gas gangrene bacillus.

Immunology

Pasteur and his team began to investigate inoculation. In 1880, they discovered how to vaccinate chickens against chicken cholera. In 1881, Pasteur discovered how to attenuate (weaken) the anthrax bacillus by heating it.

Pasteur had proved that he could inoculate animals, but what about human beings? In 1885, while he was developing an inoculation against rabies, an opportunity presented itself to find out: a 9-year-old boy called Joseph Meister had been bitten by a rabid dog. With nothing to lose, Pasteur inoculated the boy, who survived not only the dog bite, but also injection with a virulent form of the disease.

Pasteur knew that the Ukrainian zoologist Elie Metchnikoff, studying starfish, had investigated what he called "innate immunity"—that the starfish's white blood cells (the "phagocytes") seemed to be able to attack and ingest certain harmful microbes. In 1887, Pasteur brought Metchnikoff to a new laboratory at the Pasteur Institute to research how people might be given "acquired immunity."

With typical showmanship, Pasteur set up a demonstration of his anthrax vaccine at Pouilly-le-Fort, in France, using a flock of sheep. He inoculated 25 sheep and then, a fortnight later, gave anthrax to the whole flock. On June 2, Pasteur invited a group of journalists to witness—as he had predicted—the last un-inoculated sheep die, whilst "the 25 inoculated animals frolicked and gave signs of perfect health."

Is vaccination a dead end?

A number of successful vaccines were produced. In the 1890s, the British bacteriologist Almroth Wright produced vaccines against typhoid and pneumonia. Then, in 1906, two French microbiologists, Albert Calmette and Camille Guerin, developed the *Bacille Calmette-Guerin* (BCG) vaccine, which every school-age child is still given today to protect them against tuberculosis.

So was vaccination the solution to the problem of disease? It seemed that all that was needed was to take some dead or weakened germs, inject them into the patient, and let the body learn how to defend itself.

However, back in 1890, Robert Koch had launched "tuberculin," a supposed vaccine for tuberculosis, and it did not work. Then, in the 1920s, many of the vaccines produced by Almroth Wright—supposedly able to combat boils, colds, flu, sore throats, upset stomachs, catarrh and cancer—turned out to be failures. Although some vaccinations proved successful, clearly there were diseases that the human body could not defend itself against.

School textbooks relate how the young French doctor Charles Chamberland—one of Pasteur's researchers—discovered immunization when he injected some chickens with an old culture of germs. Although the story may be true, it oversimplifies the story of the development of immunology, which Pasteur and his team had been investigating for a number of years.

Anti-bodies

The Germans developed the ideas of the French. In 1890, Emil Behring and Shibasaburo Kitasato—two members of Koch's research team in Berlin—discovered that a diphtheria patient could recover if given a blood serum from animals that had recovered from the disease. Although they did not know it, they actually were giving the patient anti-bodies able to combat the disease. By 1913, they had modified this into an "anti-toxin" that could inoculate against the disease. Other serums followed that could treat tetanus, plague and cholera.

Tropical medicine

In the nineteenth century two factors led Europeans to take Western medicine to the rest of the world. First, they wanted to build up huge overseas empires and needed their administrators and soldiers to stay well. Second, missionaries wanted to take Christianity to the rest of the world and saw medicine as a way to win the hearts of the native people. In fact, after 1893, the Church Missionary Society taught medical courses as part of its missionary training. In 1876, the Scottish doctor Patrick Manson, who had worked for 23 years in the Far East, linked the disease elephantiasis to a nematode worm parasite. What was groundbreaking about this work was his study of the life-cycle of the worm, during which he discovered that the disease was transmitted by the common brown mosquito.

Manson thought that malaria might also be transmitted by an insect and in 1897 the British bacteriologist Ronald Ross identified the anopheles mosquito as the vector (carrier). Other tropical diseases were discovered to be similar: yellow fever (a virus transmitted by mosquitoes), sleeping sickness (the parasite *trypanosoma* transmitted by tsetse flies) and bilharzia (parasitical blood flukes transmitted by water snails).

In 1899, Patrick Manson founded the School of Tropical Medicine in London.

Medicine and empire

Europeans often presented conquered populations as peoples ravaged by diseases such as malaria, sleeping sickness and plague, for whom the advent of Western medicine was a blessing.

However, imperial administrations spent only a small portion of their budget on health measures, and most of their energies were devoted to keeping the white colonists, rather than the native population, healthy. The Indian nationalist Mahatma Gandhi rejected all Western medicine, seeing it as merely a means of control over the Indian people.

Yellow fever and the Panama Canal

In 1903, the United States acquired the Panama Canal Zone, and set aside $150 million to build a canal. In 1904, the first Americans arrived in Panama; by 1905, there was a yellow fever epidemic, and panic. Enter Colonel William Crawford Gorgas. He made all Westerners use mosquito nets, and sent his officials to destroy the mosquitoes. The vector (the *aëdes aegypti* mosquito) bred in small puddles of water which had collected between stones, in thrown-out tin cans and so forth. Gorgas made it an offense— punishable by a $5 fine—to allow any such environment for the larvae. Then, having deprived the mosquitoes of their usual breeding places, Gorgas had frying pans full of water put out to attract them; once they had laid their eggs the water was tipped down a disinfected drain. Local swamps were drained, and all ditches and pools covered with a layer of oil. By September 1906, the epidemic was over, and Gorgas boasted: "I have rid Panama of yellow fever— after 400 years!"

Panama, 1905: Colonel William Gorgas looks for his enemy, the mosquito.

Chapter 4

How did public health improve?

New York in the early nineteenth century

In the nineteenth century, the population of New York City grew from around 65,000 in 1800 to 3 million in 1900. Much of the increase was due to immigration from Europe, particularly large numbers of Irish rural poor, who were often ill-adapted to city life. By 1850, nearly half the city's population was foreign born.

The massive increase in population overwhelmed the public health facilities. Sewage ran down the streets, where most waste was dumped. In summer, the smell of open sewers, horse manure, tanneries, slaughterhouses, and overflowing toilets (typically shared by a dozen families) was overwhelming. The toilets were emptied exclusively by African-American workers on low wages.

Worst of all was the Five Points area where the Irish immigrants lived. The area was famous for its riots, drinking, tap dancing (a mixture of Irish jig and African dance) and its gangs, which had names like the Plug Uglies, the Slaughter Houses, and the Swamp Angels. One survey, in 1850, recorded 4,156 people living in 783 rooms. In numbers 9 and 10

Tenement life on Mulberry Street, New York, 1861.

Mulberry Street (two large 5-storey buildings) there were 69 families, numbering 357 people. Built on a former swamp, the buildings were damp with mildew, infested with rats, and a breeding ground for malaria. In a report on the filthy apartments, the *New York Daily Tribune* of June 13, 1850, commented: "There is not a farmer's hog-pen in the country that is not immeasurably ahead of them in point of health—often in point of cleanliness."

This 1881 picture from *Harper's Weekly* purports to show the conditions in New York during the cholera epidemics.

Public health improvements: local or central?

The conditions in New York were typical of urban conditions in many cities during the Industrial Revolution, and they did not cause alarm for medical reasons only. Indeed, middle class campaigners were horrified by the poverty, alcoholism, ignorance and poor morals of the working classes in the poorest areas. Poor areas were also a breeding ground for crime, violence and revolution. Thus, a number of factors lay behind the movement to improve living conditions in the cities.

Public health

In the U.S., although the federal government did undertake research, it did little practically speaking to advance public health in the nineteenth century. A National Board of Health was established in 1879, but it had little power and was abolished in 1893. Most of the key developments happened at the local level. From 1869, State Boards of Health were set up and were responsible for building sewage systems, removing public nuisances, and offering services such as free vaccination. After the 1880s, city governments provided similar services. Nevertheless, only after 1900 did the demand for greater direct federal involvement in public health increase.

The hygienists

Public health (the work of governments in preventing disease) was not the invention of the late nineteenth century, or a product of the germ theory of disease. The miasma theory (see page 20) had encouraged a "hygienic" approach to the environment, and even in the eighteenth century many European countries established "medical police" to enforce rules about hygiene, quarantine, and so forth. A number of towns in Britain applied for Acts of Parliament which allowed them to appoint medical officers, build sewers, remove nuisances and drain local swamps.

In 1799, Philadelphia built a waterworks after an outbreak of yellow fever in 1793 was blamed on the town's "noxious" drinking water. Nevertheless, despite Benjamin Rush's advocacy of regular exercise and sensible eating, the idea of hygiene was slow to establish itself in America. In 1804, the American novelist Charles Brockden Brown claimed that most Americans bathed barely once a year.

France: Louis René Villermé

Ideas about public hygiene developed in France during the Revolution. The new *écoles de santé* (see page 12) included a department of hygiene, which in the next half-century produced studies on sewerage, housing, water, industrial poisons, naval and military hygiene, gymnastics and child hygiene.

The most famous French hygienist was Louis René Villermé, who, in 1826, proved a statistical correlation between poor social conditions and high death rates.

Villermé investigated the damage modern industry did to workers' health, including that of children. This led to the 1841 French Child Labor Law.

"Filth and stench"

The pre-bacteriology hygienists fought a war against "filth and stench." Although their theory of disease was wrong, the public hygiene measures they took helped significantly to remove the environment in which disease flourished.

America: Lemuel Shattuck

Lemuel Shattuck was a teacher who became a publisher and politician. He persuaded the Massachusetts State Legislature to record births, marriages and deaths, and he designed the 1850 federal census. In 1849, he was appointed Chief Commissioner of a Sanitary Commission "to prepare and report a plan for a sanitary survey of the State." Shattuck's Report proved that in Massachusetts the poor died younger than the rich, and that most of the diseases they died from were preventable through basic hygiene.

Shattuck's recommendations, based on a study of public health provision abroad, became the basis for the Massachusetts Board of Health, the first Board of Health in America, established in 1869.

England: Edwin Chadwick

Chadwick was a barrister who was an expert on the Poor Laws. Instead of treating the symptoms of illness by giving people welfare, he tried to target the cause of disease by introducing public health measures. His *Report on the Sanitary Conditions of the Laboring Population of Great Britain* (1842) argued that the government could reduce expenditure on the poor if it spent money on public health.

The cholera epidemic of 1848–49 gave Chadwick the leverage he needed, and the Public Health Act of 1848 set up a central General Board of Health (with Chadwick in charge) with power to appoint medical officers of health, build sewers, clean streets and inspect food.

Edwin Chadwick's success was short-lived: when the cholera epidemic receded, he was dismissed (1854) and his Board of Health was abolished (1858).

Germany: Rudolf Virchow

Rudolf Virchow (see page 17) rose to fame in 1848 when the Prussian government asked him to investigate an outbreak of typhus in Silesia. He came to the conclusion that the main fault lay with a government that allowed people to live in poverty and squalor. Virchow became a life-long agitator for social reform. In 1859, he became a city councillor in Berlin, where he planned and oversaw the building of the new sewage system, two new hospitals and a school of nursing, and improved the water supply, meat inspection and school hygiene.

Florence Nightingale

Florence Nightingale, one of the most prominent and influential hygienists of the nineteenth century, achieved fame for improving the standards of cleanliness in hospitals.

In 1853, the Crimean War broke out and was disasterous. One military catastrophe of this war was commemorated by Alfred Lord Tennyson in his poem "The Charge of the Light Brigade." Moreover, it was the first war to be extensively reported in the newspapers: William Russell from *The Times* was there to record each British and French setback as it happened.

At the time, Florence Nightingale was Superintendent of the Institution for the Care of Sick Gentlewomen in Distressing Circumstances in London. Desperate for some positive press, Sidney Herbert, Minister of War, asked Florence in 1854 if she could go and help in the British Army hospital at Scutari, where wounded soldiers lay untreated and rotting along four miles of corridors. Nightingale and her team of nurses went to scrub floors and nurse the wounded. After her work

The romantic image of Florence Nightingale, "the lady with the lamp," whose shadow the soldiers were said to have kissed. In reality, her linen Turkish lamp would not have thrown enough light to make a shadow!

How successful was Florence Nightingale?

Florence Nightingale's reputation was a creation of the newspapers. In reality, the death rate at Scutari while she was in charge was higher than at any other hospital, and it was an army sanitation team that cleaned out the sewers and a French doctor who improved the food. She did not invent the idea of trained nurses (Theodore Fliedner had set up the Deaconess Institute in Germany in 1836, where Nightingale trained in 1851), and the Nightingale School for Nurses that she founded in fact trained few nurses. Provincial Nursing Associations in England did as much as Florence Nightingale to promote professionalism in nursing.

Nevertheless, though modern historians may debunk the actual achievements of Florence Nightingale herself, the principles popularized by the myth she inspired led to a radical improvement in the quality of hospital wards and nursing care throughout the world.

was reported in *The Times*, she became famous as "the lady with the lamp." For the rest of her life she used her reputation and connections to support the development of a well-trained nursing profession.

Red Cross

In 1859, a Swiss businessman called Henry Dunant found himself wandering among the wounded after the Battle of Solferino. The experience so horrified him that he set up the Red Cross to help the victims of war.

In America, Clara Barton—who bridled at being called the "American Florence Nightingale"— similarly raised money to help the huge numbers of soldiers wounded in the Civil War. In Switzerland in 1869 to recuperate from illness, Barton had the chance to meet Red Cross officials, and in 1881 she formed the American Red Cross. Indeed, it was Clara Barton who first mobilized the Red Cross for a natural calamity: the Michigan fires of 1881.

This photo of a hospital ward in New York shows a typical nursing ward of the early 1900s. Notice the high standards of hygiene and cleanliness, and the professional, uniformed nurses. The influence of army hospitals can be seen in the precise ranks of beds.

Local initiatives

After 1850, many cities introduced public health
measures on a huge scale. By 1895, every house in
Hamburg had running water. By 1900, Paris had 692
miles of sewers. In America, Massachusetts set up the
first Board of Health in 1869, followed by California in
1870. In New York City, the old system of police
department "health wardens" was replaced by a Board
of Health in 1866. In 1885, the city's Health Department
bacteriologically examined and destroyed 1,701 quarts
of milk, 72,700 pounds of sweets, 5,700 pounds of
cheese, and 4,100 pounds of coffee.

Chicago water

Chicago offers a fascinating example of a city struggling
with disease. Cholera struck every summer from 1849 to
1854. The problem was that the city got its water from
a pipe stretching 150 feet into Lake Michigan, but the
Chicago River (nicknamed "Bubbly Creek" after the
bubbles which came from the decaying waste lying on
the bottom) discharged all the city's sewage into the
lake, contaminating the water supply.

In 1851, the city set up its own waterworks (the first
municipal waterworks in America) and extended the

**Between 1856 and 1859,
London workmen moved
1 square mile of earth to lay
523 miles of sewers and
13,000 miles of drains.**

inlet pipe 600 feet into the lake, in order to get away from the pollution from the sewage. It was no use. In 1867, the city dug an underground tunnel to an inlet two miles into the lake, but this still did not work. In 1871, the city spent $3 million diverting most of the Chicago River into the Illinois and Michigan Canal. This didn't work either (the water in the canal flowed too slowly). In 1873, there was another cholera epidemic, and in the 1880s the death rate from typhoid hit 127 per 100,000 resulting in a state of emergency.

Chicago was hosting the World's Columbian Exposition of 1893, and did not like being known as "typhoid fever city." From 1892–1900, the city built the huge Sanitary and Ship Canal—25 feet deep, 160 feet wide and 28 miles long. It was so huge and so deep that it literally made the Chicago River flow backwards.

Nevertheless, Chicago's drinking water became safe only in 1906, when the water was chlorinated. In the years between 1922-1939, four sewage treatment plants were built.

Government reforms

Toward the end of the century, governments became more willing to intervene, not only with specific health measures and regulations, but also through social legislation that benefited the disadvantaged sections of society. Germany introduced sickness insurance in 1883, and both Germany and France ran public information campaigns encouraging better child-care. The British government also introduced welfare reforms, including old age pensions (1908), sickness insurance and unemployment pay (1911).

The World's Columbian Exposition of 1893 was held in Chicago, despite the problem of typhoid.

Chapter 5

What were the advances in surgery?

Surgery in the 1840s

In the early nineteenth century, American surgeons led the world. In 1809, at a time when internal surgery was still rare and dangerous in Europe, an American doctor named Dr. Ephraim McDowell—who had studied at Edinburgh University in Scotland but left without a degree—performed a successful ovariotomy on Jane Crawford, a Kentucky woman with an abdominal tumor. Although the operation took 25 minutes and was done without anesthetics, the patient lived 33 years after the operation and died at the age of 78. Philip Sang Physick, Professor of Surgery at the University of Philadelphia and known as "the father of American Surgery," not only removed gallstones successfully from dozens of patients, but also devised operations to wash out the stomach, and invented the needle forceps, a catheter and a tonsil-cutter. In 1845, Dr. James Sims developed an hour-long operation to repair the womb, usually after childbirth, now known as Sim's Operation.

Amputation—an etching (1785) by the satirical cartoonist Thomas Rowlandson —shows the horror of an amputation at the end of the eighteenth century.

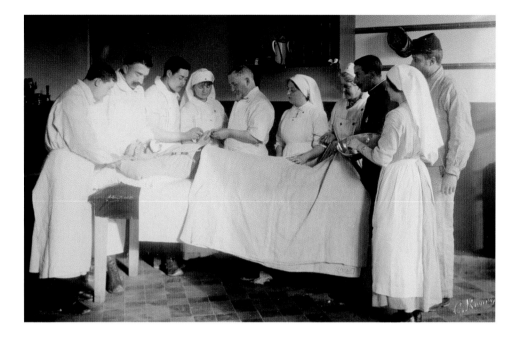

Historiography of surgery

Before the mid-eighteenth century, surgeons were generally the "poor relations" of the medical profession: setting fractures, lancing boils and removing external growths. By 1914, however, surgery was seen as a normal solution for a wide range of medical problems, and consultant surgeons were important and respected.

Early historians of medicine interpreted advances in surgery as the result of the genius of the "heroes of medicine," laying stress upon improvements in technology and the individuals who pioneered those technologies. Modern historians, however, suggest that many more issues were involved. In fact, improvements in professional prestige, new experimental surgical procedures, such as ovariotomies and Sims Operation, *pre-dated* improvements in technology and advances in anaesthesia and antiseptics.

An operation in France c. 1900. Notice the anaesthesia equipment, the clean conditions and the medical gowns of the doctor and nurses.

Carl Ruge

A German doctor, Carl Ruge, made an important breakthrough in cancer surgery when he realized that for certain cancers fewer than 50% of the people doctors operated on turned out to have cancer. In 1878, he developed the technique of biopsy, which involved studying cells from the patient to see if they were cancerous. This remains the basis of all cancer treatment today.

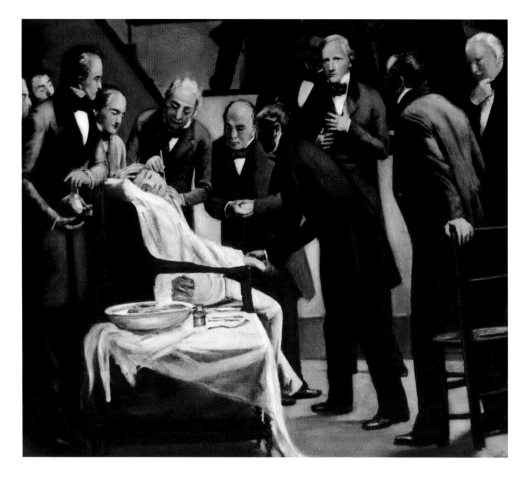

An operation before anaesthetics

Before the 1840s, surgeons did not use anaesthetics, though some had experimented with "mesmerism" (hypnotism). This is how the Victorian novelist Fanny Burney described her mastectomy in 1811. It does not make easy reading:

"When the dreadful steel was plunged into the breast – cutting through veins— arteries—flesh—nerves … I began a scream that lasted un-intermittingly during the whole time of the incision … I concluded the operation was over—Oh no! presently the terrible cutting was renewed—and worse than ever, to separate the bottom, the foundation of this dreadful gland from the parts to which it adhered … Oh heaven!—I then felt the knife against the breast bone—scraping it!"

This painting shows William T.G. Moore, left, administering anaesthesia to Gilbert Abbot while Dr. John Collins Warren removes a tumor from Abbot's neck.

The discovery of anaesthetics

Humphrey Davy had publicized the painkilling effects of nitrous oxide ("laughing gas") in 1800. It was used for entertainment in music hall shows, but only in January 1845 did an American dentist called Horace Wells use it to extract a tooth at Massachusetts General Hospital.

Three years earlier, another American dentist, William E. Clarke, had pulled a tooth using a different chemical: ether. In March 1842, the American surgeon Dr. Crawford Williamson Long used ether for an operation, and a public demonstration took place on October 16, 1846, when the American surgeon Dr. J.C. Warren removed a tumor from a man's neck.

Five days after Warren's operation, Oliver Wendell Holmes coined the term "anaesthesics" for the painkillers. By the end of the year, Robert Liston in London had amputated a leg using ether (in typical flamboyant Liston style it took him 25 seconds to saw off the leg).

After 1847, the Scottish doctor James Simpson (who so hated the pain he caused patients that he almost gave up medicine) discovered chloroform, and in 1884 the surgeon Carl Koller used cocaine as a local anaesthetic.

Dr. Crawford Williamson Long (with the knife) amputating a leg c. 1857. Notice the anaesthetist administering the ether soaked into a towel. Anaesthetics were dangerous – about 1 in every 10,000 patients died.

Acceptance of anaesthesia

Historians today do not argue, as they did in the past, about who "discovered" anaesthesia. Rather, they ask why it took surgeons so long to use substances which they had known about for 40 years. And why did Liston still operate so quickly, even though his patient was unconscious?

It took surgeons a long time to accept anaesthesia. Some doctors believed that God *intended* patients to feel pain, and some even claimed that pain made the patients try harder. Anaesthesia only really became popular after John Snow gave chloroform to Queen Victoria during the birth of her son, in 1853.

Lister and antiseptics

In 1927, Dr. John Leeson remembered his days as a medical student in London in 1871, before surgeons understood anything about germs:

"I remember the house-surgeon in the theatre with his threaded needles dangling from the front flap of his coat ... An operation was a dirty job and an outworn old coat was a suitable garment! I see it now, faded with age, stained with blood and spotted with pus."

There was little excuse for this state of affairs. In 1843, Oliver Wendell Holmes had noticed that deaths from puerperal fever (among women who had given birth) fell markedly if doctors washed their hands in a solution of chloride of lime before they moved to attend a new patient. Then in 1865, Joseph Lister, professor of Surgery at Glasgow University, learned about Pasteur's theory of germs. He used a carbolic acid spray to disinfect his operations and the patients' wounds, and his post-operative mortality rate fell from 46 per cent to

Anaesthetics allowed surgeons to perform much longer, much more complicated operations inside the human body. In 1881, the German surgeon Theodor Billroth (shown here) successfully operated on a patient's stomach.

15 per cent. Lister's "antiseptic surgery" meant that for the first time in history, patients could go to the hospital to have an operation with the expectation that they would get better, instead of being fearful of disease.

As the century progressed, surgeons attempted ever more adventurous operations. They learned how to go into the body, cut out the affected part, and then repair the tissues (this is called "resective surgery"). By the first decade of the twentieth century, surgeons were experimenting – sometimes successfully – with transplants of organs such as pancreases, testicles and ovaries.

Opposition to antiseptics

Early medical historians saw Lister as the founder of a new age. In fact, when he moved to King's College London, he generally met with a hostile reception. One lecturer had a standard joke, telling students who failed to shut the door to do so quickly, lest one of Mr. Lister's germs came in! Few doctors at that time believed in the germ theory. Surgeons did not like being told that they were causing their patients' deaths. The nurses also felt that Lister was implying that they were not keeping the wards clean.

Lister's carbolic spray soon fell out of use. By the 1880s, surgeons were developing instead "aseptic surgery"—operating under sterile conditions. In 1890, the American surgeon William Halsted introduced the use of rubber gloves during surgery and, seven years later, German surgeons started using face masks.

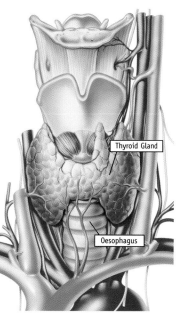

Thyroid Gland

Oesophagus

The Swiss surgeon Theodor Kocher discovered that when he removed the thyroid gland (pictured here), his patients fell ill. So, in 1883, he tried replacing it with thyroid tissue from another person: the first ever transplant.

Hospital beds

In the early nineteenth century, there were no operations which were specific to hospitals. Minor operations, such as tonsillectomies, continued to be done in people's homes and doctors' surgeries well into the twentieth century. However, the development of intricate and internal operations towards the end of the nineteenth century established the hospital as the place where you went to have an operation. In America, the number of hospitals rose from 100 in 1870 to more than 4,000 by the early twentieth century.

Chapter 6

How did treatment improve?

The end of the old

Towards the end of the eighteenth century, doctors had begun to question treatments based on the theory of the four humors. French doctors led the way. In the 1800s, Pierre Louis, who became *Interne des Hôpitaux de Paris* (Resident Physician of the Hospitals of Paris) in 1823, proved that bleeding patients did not cure pneumonia. Doctors began instead to investigate whether there were any drugs or chemicals that would cure or alleviate disease, including substances such as strychnine (a poison used as a stimulant), quinine (a drug which cured malaria), morphine and codeine (painkillers).

Magic bullets

The work of Pasteur and Koch on germs further encouraged doctors to continue looking for cures. The German bacteriologist Paul Ehrlich (1854–1915) investigated the effects of chemical dyes. If certain dyes could

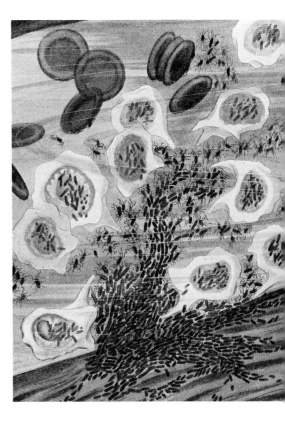

This picture from 1912—entitled *Health and Disease in Deadly Combat*—shows, in a drop of blood, "the wonderful white cells attacking, swallowing, killing, digesting the black parasites which mean disease."

Flu pandemic

Despite all the developments in medicine in the nineteenth century, there was still little doctors could do when faced with infectious disease.

In 1918, American soldiers training in the US began to catch flu. From there it spread to France and to Spain—where people began to call it Spanish flu—and then all over the world. A fifth of the population of the world caught the Spanish flu, and more than 20 million people died of it. It was the worst pandemic of all time.

stain certain bacteria, then perhaps there were dyes that could kill them? Two proved successful: methylene blue, which attacked the malaria parasite, and trypan red, which attacked *trypanosoma*, the parasite that caused sleeping sickness.

Consequently, Ehrlich began to try other chemicals. In 1889, he set up a private laboratory and assembled a research team. In 1909, after thousands of tests, his assistant, Sahachiro Hata, at last discovered that chemical number 606 (an arsenic compound called salvarsan) cured syphilis. Chemical solutions, also called "magic bullets," were hard to find, however, and no others were discovered until the 1930s.

In 1893, the Danish doctor Niels Finsen found that ultraviolet light killed the tuberculosis bacilli in skin lesions. Dozens of sanatoria opened in the Alps, where tuberculosis patients spent hours sunbathing in the fresh air. Sanatoria were also established in America; the first was built by Edward Trudeau at Saranac Lake in the mountains north of New York.

New technology

What about other modern discoveries? Could they perhaps help patients? Doctors tried magnetism, and tortured their patients with electricity. They injected them with animal hormones and extracts of guinea pig and dogs' testicles. More successfully, by 1900, doctors also had started to use radium (discovered only two years earlier by Marie and Pierre Curie) in the treatment of cancer.

A medical profession

There were significant improvements in both the quality and popular perception of doctors during the nineteenth century.

The quality of medical education improved greatly during the century. Some universities established medical schools at this time, although many had already been established years before. Universities sponsored research and hospital practice, improved student discipline and set meaningful examinations. In America, in 1910, Abraham Flexner surveyed 157 different medical schools and found many of them unsatisfactory. Several schools were forced to close down simply because they were unable to afford the required

A LUCID INTERVAL.

In this *Punch* cartoon of 1891, the maid is telling the doctor: "Well—he has been wandering a good deal in his mind. Early this morning I think I heard him say, 'what an old woman that doctor is!'—and I think that was about the last really rational remark he made." The cartoon pokes fun at the doctor, but he appears to be concerned, smartly-dressed and well-to-do. There is none of the vicious hostility shown in the eighteenth century caricatures of Hogarth (see page 4) and Rowlandson (see page 38).

facilities. By the end of the nineteenth century, there were practitioners without university training still practicing medicine, but they were regarded by everybody as being of low status.

A code of ethics

Better training was connected to an improvement in professional behavior. The first book on medical ethics was published by Thomas Percival, in 1803. Many others followed, and ethics became an important part of every university course. The forerunner to the British Medical Association was founded in 1832, the American Medical Association in 1847 and the French Association *Générale de Médecins* in 1858. In Germany, doctors formed local associations called *Ärztekammer*. These associations encouraged doctors to meet socially and professionally, and some of them enforced codes of ethics. At the same time, learned journals such as *The Lancet* (1823) and, in America, the *Medical Repository* campaigned for better standards and transmitted new research to ordinary doctors.

Doctors in 1800 were widely criticized. This Thomas Rowlandson cartoon is called "Medical Dispatch" or "Doctor Doubledose Killing Two Birds with One Stone," and shows a doctor neglecting his patient while he flirts with her daughter.

Hospital medicine

In the 1970s, the medical historian Nicholas Jewson argued that the nineteenth century saw the replacement of the old "bedside medicine" (which concentrated on how the disease would develop and relieving the symptoms) with "hospital medicine" (which concentrated on the diagnosis and classification of the disease). This, he argued, may have helped the progress of medicine but meant that the patient was treated as a "case," particularly in the use of technical jargon, rather than as a person.

Women doctors

In Europe in the nineteenth century, women were forbidden to become doctors and had to fight to enter this male-oriented profession. Women were not allowed to study to become doctors anywhere in Europe before the 1860s, and not in Belgium, Norway, Spain or Portugal until the 1880s. In Britain, Sophia Jex-Blake founded the London School of Medicine for Women in 1874, and the British Parliament allowed women to qualify as doctors in 1876.

By contrast, in America, many women were actively engaged in the medical profession in the nineteenth century. They worked as midwives (where they were preferred to male doctors), nurses and doctors. As the century progressed, women's medical colleges and women's hospitals were established: Dr Lucy Sewell, resident physician at the New England Hospital for Women, was Sophia Jex-Blake's inspiration. In 1900, there were 7,000 female doctors in America. The only other country that welcomed female doctors was Russia (which had more than 1,600 in 1913).

Sophia Jex-Blake went to Edinburgh University after she was rejected by London University. She was obliged to take separate classes from the male students and after she had passed the exams, the University would not grant her a degree, only a "certificate of proficiency" (which would not have allowed her to practice as a doctor). In the end, she got a degree in Switzerland and her license to practice medicine in Ireland.

Elizabeth Garrett attended classes in London hospitals, went to court to force the university to allow her to take the exam, and then acquired a license from the Society of Apothecaries (which did not have rules excluding women). In 1866, she set up the St. Mary's Dispensary for Women, and in 1873, managed to be admitted to the British Medical Association.

Women excluded

Historians used to present the acceptance of female doctors as a successful struggle by certain key female pioneers such as Elizabeth Blackwell, Elizabeth Garrett and Sophia Jex-Blake. Recently, however, this view has been questioned. In fact, few women became doctors, and opposition remained fierce. As late as 1911, there were only 495 women on the Medical Register in Britain and there were only 138 women doctors in Germany in 1913.

In America, women doctors were faced with increasing male sexism, which eventually drove them out of the profession. The Flexner Report of 1910 forced the small women's medical schools to close, and the American Medical Association did not admit women until 1915. Although women were still allowed to work as nurses and assistants in medical laboratories, where they did not threaten men's control of the profession, the number of women doctors plummeted.

Modern feminist historians have pointed out that getting women into the medical profession involved more than changing a few rules: the whole structure of society—for example girls' education, parental attitudes and institutional sexism—worked against women becoming doctors, even when they were allowed to do so by law.

Elizabeth Blackwell **obtained a medical degree in America, and set up the New York Infirmary for Indigent Women (1857). Returning to Britain, she was accepted onto the Medical Register in 1858.**

The role of women

Women were said to be unsuitable for doctoring (or work of any kind) because, as the *Manual of Midwifery* (1828) put it, they are "subservient to reproduction":

"Her destiny is to be united to a husband and to become a mother...Women are more liable to diseases than the other sex. The constitution is more feeble, peculiarly influenced by the mysterious process of reproduction."

Doctors believed that over-exercise would divert energy from the womb, leading to sterility, sickness and hysteria (the word "hysteria" comes from the Greek word meaning "womb").

The Modern Physician

The book *The Modern Physician* (1910), by Dr. Andrew Wilson, gives us an idea of what professional medicine was like for ordinary people at the turn of the century.

Dr. Wilson complains about the "quacks" who flooded the newspapers of the time with advertisements for their "so-called cures." Then he lists the kind of drugs "most likely to be of service in a household." These included a number of chemical substances. For instance, he tells us that sulphuric acid is a tonic, arsenic in water can help skin diseases, and different preparations of ammonia are useful for liver complaints, neuralgia and nervous troubles. Other substances patients are recommended to swallow include alcohol, caffeine, cocaine, iron, mercury, saltpetre, opium, rhubarb, creosote and extract of the thyroid gland. (Most of these are more likely to harm than to heal.)

In this *Punch* cartoon from 1869, a doctor visits a fashionable patient. She says: "Cod-liver oil! I couldn't take such horrible stuff as that."He replies: "Well, what would you say to a cream and orange liqueur?" Despite all the advances in medicine, general practitioners could do very little to cure sickness, and their role remained primarily to alleviate symptoms and reassure patients.

Useful recipes

Dr. Wilson's section on "Useful Recipes" illustrates the kinds of home-medicine that ordinary people might use. A starch poultice could be smeared on the crusts of skin diseases. A burn could be dressed with a liniment made from olive oil, belladonna and chloroform. There are lotions for eczema and ringworm, and a number of powders, pills and mixtures for chest and stomach complaints. One recipe for constipation was made of aloes, strychnine and soap, and a diarrhoea recipe was made of chalk powder, bicarbonate of soda, chloroform and peppermint water.

There is a long section on nursing, and a detailed chapter on "cooking for invalids," since "in many cases invalids are more dependent on food than on medicine." Wilson advises that cooks should be "exquisitely clean" and that meals should be recently prepared using fresh ingredients. The kind of meals he recommends for patients include chicken broth, fish omelette, stewed tripe, arrowroot pudding and oatmeal gruel.

It is significant that none of the "recipes" are described as "cures," and the reader is left with the impression that many patients had no hope of getting better. In 1910, doctors could make the patient comfortable and relieve some of the symptoms, but the body had to heal itself—or the person died or remained an invalid.

The Philadephia firm selling these quack remedies promised the public that "brighter hours will come" with the use of their medicines, which included pulmonary syrup, itch ointment and a piles remedy.

A great invention in health?

Part of the improvement in health in the nineteenth century had nothing to do with medicine, but was due to changes in the way people lived. The invention of the rubber condom (thought to have taken place in America in the 1870s) was especially important for women's health, as it stopped the spread of sexually transmitted diseases. It also meant that the mortality rate from childbirth declined as, overall, women had fewer pregnancies.

The playwright George Bernard Shaw called the rubber condom the "greatest invention of the nineteenth century."

Untrained healers

The powerlessness of doctors to fight disease, and the fact that their fees were far too high for ordinary people, led many people to turn to "quacks" (untrained healers). In Britain, in 1854, it was estimated that there were 6,000 such men.

Some popular movements rejected professional medicine altogether, while appealing to the new "scientific" ideas of the time. Franz Anton Mesmer (1734–1815) and his followers claimed to cure patients by "mesmerism" (hypnotism). Similarly, Samuel Hahnemann of Vienna (1755–1843) held that infinitesimal doses of poisons and metals kept the body healthy. This idea was called homeopathy.

Most alternative medicines advocated personal hygiene and used "natural cures" in some form or another. The American healer Samuel S. Thomson (1769–1843) advocated herbal cures, particularly use of the plant known as "Indian tobacco," which caused vomiting and sweating. Vincent Priessnitz (1799–1851) of Vienna developed "hydropathy" (water treatment), including vapor baths, brine baths and sulphur baths. Mary Baker Eddy (1821–1910), founder of the Christian Science religion, taught that the physical world,

Lydia E. Pinkham's Vegetable Compound—promoted as a cure for a range of female complaints from dizziness to menopause—sold so well that "Lilly the Pink" became America's first female millionaire. This 1949 photo shows its ingredients: unicorn root, pleurisy root, black cohosh, fenugreek and a large amount of alcohol. It is now believed that black cohosh affects the serotonin (a chemical influencing mood) level in the brain.

Alternative medicine

Many nineteenth century alternative medicines still survive today. "Osteopaths," who believe that the health of the body is affected by mechanical disturbances, and "chiropractors," who manipulate the spine and other body systems to maintain good health, continue to practice and are even a standard feature of contemporary healthcare options.

including disease and pain, was illusory. She advocated "mind over matter" and the cure of "disease" by faith alone.

The American Sylvester Graham (1795-1851) and his "Grahamites" thought that sexual lust endangered health. He recommended hard mattresses, cold showers, vegetarianism and high fiber cereals. To this end he invented "Graham Crackers," a kind of digestive biscuit made from whole wheat flour.

Sequah, the great healer

The famous "quack" William Henry Harley (known as "the Great Seqah") worked in Britain from 1887–1895. Preceded by a brass band, dressed as a cowboy and surrounded by "Red Indians," "Sequah" would start by pulling out dozens of bad teeth at immense speed, much to the crowd's delight. Then, after a short speech on the failures of modern medicine (while medical students shouted "Science against quackery!"), he would sell his "Prairie Flower Oil," a rheumatism cure supposedly made from herbs and mineral water found only in the Wild West (chemical analysis showed that it contained aloes, potash and alcohol). He was so successful that by 1890 there were 23 Sequahs working all over Britain and Ireland, and Sequah Ltd. had been floated as a public company, with a share capital four times that of the country's biggest chemist.

In 1866, a religious group called the Seventh Day Adventists set up an alternative medicine "Health Reform Institute" in Michigan. Their "gospel of health" advocated a lifestyle based on hydropathy and roughage. Around 1894, as part of this regime, Will Keith Kellogg, brother of the Head of the Institute, rolled out a mash of maize and turned it into corn flakes.

Let our Sweetheart be your Sweetheart

The sweetheart of the corn

TOASTED CORN FLAKES

Have you tried it in winter with hot milk? It's delicious.

Look for this signature *W. K. Kellogg*

Toasted Corn Flake Company, Battle Creek, Mich.

Mental health in the nineteenth century

Before the nineteenth century, people with any mental illness or congenital disorder, such as Down's Syndrome, were usually put together in a madhouse with alcoholics, syphilitics and the criminally insane.

However, during the French Revolution, Philippe Pinel, who had been put in charge of the Paris asylum, found that kindness and counselling could help mental health patients. In the nineteenth century in America, a number of asylums were built where the ideal was "moral management." The idea came from the York Retreat, an asylum which was set up in 1796 in England by a group of Quakers. There "neither chains nor corporal punishment are tolerated," and treatments included role play, occupational therapy, and establishing a family-like atmosphere.

Such treatments, however, still proved to be ineffective, and investigators, such as the New England social reformer Dorothea Dix (1802–1887), discovered that in many asylums mentally ill patients continued to be treated badly. Benjamin Rush, who was in charge of the mental patients at Philadelphia Hospital for 30 years, invented a "tranquilizing chair" as an improvement over previous methods of restraint, but with the patient strapped by wrists, feet and chest, and

Hogarth's engraving of Bedlam asylum, based on an actual visit he made in *c.* 1735, gives an idea of how bizarre and often horrific such places were.

with a wooden box over his head, such an approach would today be regarded as criminal malpractice.

The development of psychiatry

In 1779, the Edinburgh doctor William Cullen defined insanity not as a disease, but as a nervous disorder originating in the brain. This was an important development, because if mental illness was not a disease, then it did not need treatment by doctors. In the nineteenth century, however, doctors began to claim control over mental as well as physical illnesses. The German psychiatrist Wilhelm Griesinger (1817–1868) asserted that "psychological diseases are diseases of the brain... insanity is only a symptom."

As the century progressed, Benedict Morel (1809–1873) and Henry Maudsley (1835–1918) linked psychiatry with Darwin's ideas about evolution. Mental illness, they said, was "degenerative" and linked to heredity or depraved behavior (such as alcoholism or masturbation). The Italian criminologist Cesare Lombroso (1836–1909) linked degeneration to identifiable physical traits such as low brows and jutting jaws.

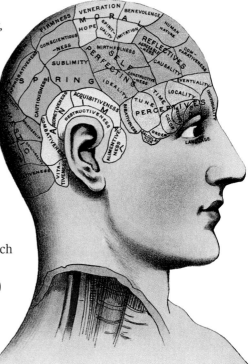

Franz Josef Gall (1758–1828) claimed that different mental faculties were located in different parts of the brain. His theory of phrenology (judging mental health by the lumps on the skull) is now discredited, but it was a very popular theory in the nineteenth century.

Mental illness

Treatments for mental illness in the later nineteenth century included: straight-jackets, terror (such as being whipped with nettles, submersed in a tub of eels, or bound in "the whirling chair"), hypnotism, regression therapy, cold shower-baths, removal (for women) of the womb or ovaries, lobotomy (after 1890) and increasingly, tranquilizers, such as chloral hydrate and morphia.

Although treatments remained incredibly cruel long into the twentieth century, the gradual development of hospital care, and the attempts of doctors such as Sigmund Freud to try to understand and treat mental illness, nevertheless laid the foundations of modern psychiatry and mental health care.

Chapter 7

How successful was nineteenth century medicine?

Modern medicine

"Modern medicine, by which I mean 'our' medicine, was the product of nineteenth-century society," writes the medical historian W.F. Bynum, and it would be easy to represent the nineteenth century as a time of continuous and significant progress in the history of medicine.

The previous chapters have documented many fundamental medical advances: experimental physiology, cell theory, germ theory, bacteriology and immunization, hygiene and public health, anaesthesia, antiseptics and nursing, and numerous advances in medical technology, from the stethoscope to the electrocardiograph. These developments turned out to be the foundation needed for the progress of medicine in the twentieth century.

At the same time, there was a parallel improvement in the skills of doctors and the prestige of the medical profession. The respectable hospital consultant physicians of the early twentieth century were a world away from the doctors of the eighteenth century, who were stoned by the mob as they fled London to get

This painting, by the Victorian artist Luke Fildes, shows a compassionate but powerless doctor watching a sick child. A bottle of medicine and a cup sit useless on the table. The painting was inspired by Fildes' experience of the care given to his own son, Phillip, by their family doctor. This painting helped to improve the public perception of the medical profession, and many doctors hung a copy of it in their waiting rooms. In actuality, however, poor people such as this family would never have been able to afford a proper doctor.

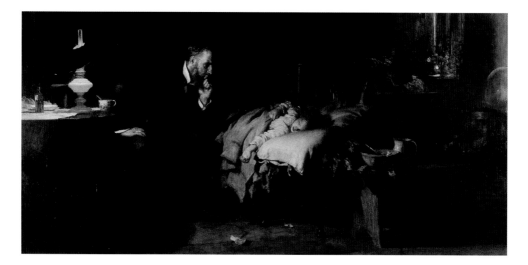

away from the plague. The nineteenth century's" heroes of health" are still famous today, and some of their names have even entered our vocabulary—milk is said to be "pasteurized" and there is an antiseptic mouthwash called "Listerine."

"A box of blanks"

Yet, for all the advances of the nineteenth century, doctors remained largely unable to cure disease. They carried, as the medical historian Roy Porter has called it, "a box of blanks." "Had a [bubonic plague] epidemic occurred in western Europe at any time before 1939," comments the medical historian F.F. Cartwright, "physicians would have been as helpless to cure their patients as were doctors in the Black Death."

At the end of the nineteenth century, despite the advances in bacteriology and immunology, when faced with serious illness, doctors remained largely unable to cure infectious disease.

During the nineteenth century pharmaceutical firms grew up such as Bayer in Germany (1863) and Burroughs Wellcome & Co. in America (1880). In 1898, Bayer invented a morphine-based cough syrup which they claimed would be non-addictive; they called it "heroin."

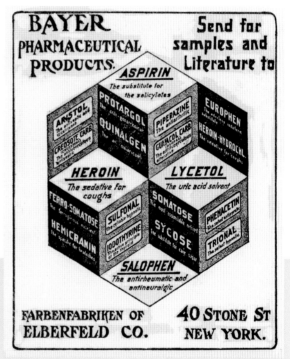

Deadly painkillers

Although painkillers are one of the greatest benefits of nineteenth century medicine, addiction was a terrible side-effect. The opium-based drug laudanum, used for headaches and to soothe crying babies, was freely available. Famous laudanum addicts included the poet Coleridge, the anti-slavery campaigner Wilberforce, King George IV of England and Wyatt Earp's wife, Mattie. Thousands of soldiers became addicted to morphine, another opium-based painkiller, during the American Civil War.

In America, in 1886, a Dr. John Stith Pemberton invented a soft drink called Coca-Cola to help morphine addicts quit. It was made from coca plants and cola nuts, and contained cocaine and caffeine.

Typhoid Mary

Despite the developments and inventions of the nineteenth century, disease was still a terrifying and sinister enemy. The case of "typhoid Mary" illustrates just how vulnerable society was.

Mary Mallon in the hospital. The doctors gave her urotopin —an antiseptic for the urinary tract—but, of course, it was useless; the antibiotics that could have cured her were not available for another 30 years.

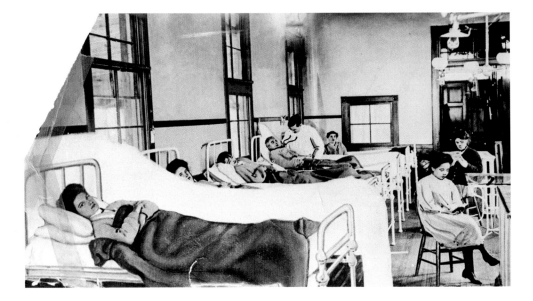

Mary Mallon was an Irish immigrant in New York State who worked as a cook. She had eight jobs in seven years, and in seven of those families there were outbreaks of typhoid, a disease of the bowels (the bacterium which causes it, *salmonella typhi*, is passed on in food). In 1907, health officials tracked these outbreaks back to Mary. She had recovered from the disease, but was a carrier of the bacillus.

The idea of a "carrier" was new in the 1900s and at first Mary was quarantined for two years in a hospital for communicable diseases. She complained that "there was never any effort to do anything for

Toothpaste

Better health often requires changes in personal habits. In 1873, the Colgate company started selling Colgate Dental Cream. It came in a jar, smelled nice, and tasted much better than charcoal or soap, which was what most people used. In 1896, Colgate introduced the squeezable tube. People started cleaning their teeth more effectively, and this helped reduce the problem of dental decay.

Levi Spear Parmly (1790-1859), a New Orleans dentist, is credited as the inventor of modern dental floss. Parmly promoted flossing with a piece of silk thread in 1815.

me excepting to keep me a prisoner without being sick."
She was, she alleged, being kept there merely as "a
peep show for everybody."

In 1910, Mary was released on condition that she never work as a cook again. She disappeared and was only rediscovered in 1915, working as a cook at a women's hospital, when an outbreak of typhoid killed two of the patients there. Mary stayed unnoticed for so long because typhoid was such a common disease in the industrial towns and cities of the time.

Standards of living

Nevertheless, there is no doubt that by looking at measures such as the death rate and life expectancy people seem to have become healthier by the end of the nineteenth century. In 1976, Dr. Thomas McKeown argued that this was due to improvements in the standard of living, and the benefits of facilities such as gas, electricity and plumbing. Although more recently historians have argued that hospitals, and particularly public health measures, also played a part, it does seem that a wealthier population, better fed and better educated in hygienic habits, was more able to avoid illness. Thus, it is arguable that the Industrial Revolution largely solved the health problems it created, and the general improvement in health stemmed from a healthier environment rather than from improvements in curative medicine.

The *real* improvements in curative medicine were waiting for the doctors and scientists of the twentieth century.

Just as important as the public hygiene measures of the nineteenth century was the gradual infiltration into the home of ideas about hygiene. Advertisements encouraged housewives to buy products such as soap and disinfectants. In the 1880s, companies began to claim that their products not only removed dirt and smells, but also killed germs.

Glossary

Acute infection a disease (e.g. a cold) which develops quickly but from which you can "get better," as opposed to chronic illness.

Aetiology the investigation of the causes and the progress of diseases.

Amputation cutting off a diseased or damaged limb.

Anaesthetics pain-killers.

Anatomy the study of the structure and parts of the body.

Antibodies cells in the body which identify, attack and kill germs.

Antiseptics chemicals which kill germs.

Aseptic germ-free.

Asylum a "place of safety," used to name the place where mentally ill people were incarcerated.

Attenuated weakened.

Autopsy the dissection of a dead body, usually to establish the precise cause of death.

Bacilli (singular: bacillus) bacteria.

Bacteria Microscopic single-cell organisms lacking a nucleus, which can cause disease.

Bacteriologists the German term for researchers who study microbes.

Biopsy the removal of a small section of tissue from the body so that the cells can be studied in order to reach a diagnosis.

Cardio-vascular body systems associated with the heart and veins.

Carrier a person with an infectious disease (who may not demonstrate any symptoms) who infects others.

Chemotherapy treating diseases with drugs.

Chiropractic alternative theory of medicine which claimed to cure illnesses by manipulating the back.

Chronic illness a long-term condition (e.g. arthritis).

Congenital a disease present at birth and usually (though not necessarily) genetic.

Degenerative in the sense it was used in nineteenth century medicine, this referred to any condition which doctors saw as a genetic deterioration to a less highly-evolved type.

Democracy a system where people elect their government.

Diagnosis the assessment of what illness a person has.

Electrocardiograph a machine which monitors the heart.

Endemic a disease which is continuously present in the population (e.g. tuberculosis).

Epidemic a sudden large-scale outbreak of a disease (e.g. cholera).

Ethics the moral code for a profession.

Eugenics a movement that wished to remove "defective" or "degenerative" genes from the human race, usually by sterilization.

Germ theory the theory that diseases are caused by germs.

Heredity where traits are handed down from one generation to the next in a person's genes.

Histology the visual study of cells to identify diseases and cancers.

Homeopathy alternative theory of medicine, which holds that taking poisons in tiny quantities preserves health.

Hormones chemical secretions from glands (e.g. thyroid, pituitary, adrenal, pancreas), which control how the body functions.

Humoral pathology the belief that health and the human body are controlled by the "four humors" (blood, phlegm, yellow bile and black bile).

Hydropathy an alternative theory of medicine which advocates the use of water in health treatments.

Imbecile a nineteenth century word for a person of low intelligence.

Immune system the body systems that resist diseases.

Inoculation an injection with a substance (usually an attenuated form of a disease) so that the body can gain immunity to that disease.

Kymograph a machine which measures the pulse.

Legislation the act or process of making laws.

Lobotomy an operation which severs the frontal lobes of the brain from the rest of the brain.

Lunatic a nineteenth century word for a person who is mentally ill.

Magic bullet Paul Ehrlich's term for antibodies.

Medical police an eighteenth century term denoting laws made to improve the public health.

Medicaments a nineteenth century word for medicines.

Menopause the time when a woman's body ceases to be able to have a baby.

Mesmerism a nineteenth century term for hypnotism, coined after its populariser, Friedrich Mesmer.

Miasma an eighteenth/nineteenth century term meaning a disease-bearing bad smell.

Microbiologists the French term for researchers who study microbes.

Midwives women who attend at childbirth.

Mortality rate death rate.

Obstetrics area of medicine concerned with pregnancy and childbirth.

Osteopathy alternative theory of medicine which claimed to cure illnesses by manipulating the bones, especially the back.

Pandemic an epidemic which spreads through a number of countries.

Parasite a plant or animal which lives on another organism, usually causing disease or the death of the host.

Pasteurization the process of heating a liquid (e.g. milk) to kill the germs so that it lasts longer before it turns.

Pathology the study of what causes diseases and how this affects the human body.

Phagocyte a type of white blood cell which can engulf and destroy a germ inside the body.

Phrenology a system, now discredited, which held that the shape of the skull allowed doctors to diagnose mental traits and illnesses.

Physiology the study of how the body works.

Psychology the study of human behavior, particularly insanity and mental health.

Public health the measures taken by the government to control health and disease.

Quacks unregistered healers (and, by implication, charlatans).

Quarantine isolation of people who have, or are suspected of having, an infectious disease.

Reductionism the idea that the human body is merely a series of physical and chemical reactions and involves no special "spirit" or "soul."

Resective surgery cutting out part of the body, then repairing the remaining tissues.

Sanatorium an institution for the treatment of invalids and the chronically ill (tuberculosis patients).

Sanitation a system of drains, sewers and water pipes.

Scavengers people employed in the nineteenth century to collect refuse and sewage.

Socialism a political theory which believes that the state should own all the means of production, and use them for the benefit of all people equally in a classless society.

Spontaneous generation the erroneous pre-Pasteur theory that disease created bacteria (whereas today we know that the opposite is true).

Surgery medical operations on patients.

Vaccination a term coined by Pasteur in honor of Jenner, meaning inoculation.

Variolation the procedure, common before 1800, of infecting children with a weak form of smallpox in the hope that they would gain immunity to the disease.

Vitamin an organic compound essential for the normal functioning of the body.

Vivisection the dissection of an animal or human being while they are still alive.

Timeline

Breakthrough dates in the history of 19th century medicine

Events	Dates	People
	1790	1796 Edward Jenner demonstrates vaccination for smallpox.
	1800	1803 Thomas Percival publishes his book on medical ethics.
	1820	1826 Joseph Jackson Lister invents the achromatic microscope lens.
		1829 Louis Villermé introduces statistical methods into public health research.
		1834 Pierre Louis suggests that changes inside the body are more important in diagnosis than outward symptoms.
		1839 Theodor Schwann shows that all tissue is comprised of cells, not humors.
	1840	1842 Crawford Williamson Long uses ether as an anaesthetic in surgery.
1847 Reductionism: German doctors declare that the processes of the human body are merely chemical reactions.		1848 Edwin Chadwick sets up the first Board of Health.
		1854 John Snow disconnects the Broad Street pump, proving that cholera is not caused by a miasma.
	1860	1863 Henri Dunant sets up the Red Cross.
1876 An Act of Parliament allows women to qualify as doctors in Britain.		1867 Joseph Lister's research on antiseptic surgery is published in The Lancet.
	1880	1882 Robert Koch demonstrates the tuberculosis bacillus before the Berlin Physiological Society.
		1895 Wilhelm Röntgen discovers X-rays.
	1900	1902 Starling and Bayliss discover the first hormone.
		1906 Calmette and Guerin develop the BCG vaccine against tuberculosis.
1910 The Flexner Report establishes the standards for medcal schools in America.	1910	1909 Paul Ehrlich's team develop Salvarsan 606 as a cure for syphilis.

Further information

Books

Phil Gates, *History News: Medicine News* (Candlewick, 2000)

Gael Jennings, *Bloody Moments: And Further Highlights from the History of Medicine* (Annick Press, 2000)

Nick Arnold, *Microscopic Monsters and Deadly Diseases* (Gardners Books, 2004)

Children's histories concentrating on the gruesome bits.

Jeanette Farrell, *Invisible Enemies: Stories of Infectious Disease* (Farrar, Straus & Giroux, 2005)

Albert Marrin, *Dr. Jenner and the Speckled Monster: the Search for the Smallpox Vaccine* (Dutton Books, 2002)

Steve Parker, *Eyewitness: Medicine* (DK Children, 2000)

Books for older children

Roy Porter, *Blood and Guts: A Short History of Medicine* (W. W. Norton, 2003)

Roy Porter, *Quacks: Fakers & Charlatans in English Medicine* (Tempus, 2003)

James H Cassedy, *Medicine in America: A Short History* (John Hopkins University Press, 1991)

Roy Porter (editor), *The Cambridge Illustrated History of Medicine* (Cambridge, 2001)

Julie M. Fenster, *Ether Day: The Strange Tale of America's Greatest Medical Discovery and the Haunted Men Who Made It* (HarperCollins, 2001)

Ira Rutkow, *Bleeding Blue and Gray: Civil War Surgery and the Evolution of American Medicine* (Random House, 2005)

Books for young adults.

Websites

http://www.bbc.co.uk/history/discovery/ medicine/
Deals simply with advances in medicine, Florence Nightingale, and the battle against smallpox.

http://www.historylearningsite.co.uk/history_ of_medicine.htm
Clear, informative site for young students.

http://www.schoolshistory.org.uk/ infectiousdisease.htm
A site following British school curricula, which offers a hyperlink way through the subject.

http://www.historyworld.net/
A collection of illustrated timelines on Birth, Death, Drugs, Hospitals, Plagues, Surgery and Technology. Go through Timelines link, or search by "medicine through time."

http://www.ihm.nlm.nih.gov/
Gateway to the US National Library of Medicine. Nearly 60,000 images in a variety of media illustrating the social and historically specific aspects of medicine.

http://www.library.ucla.edu/libraries/biomed/ his/painexhibit/
Academic but clear site about anaesthesia.

http://www.healthsystem.virginia.edu/internet/ library/historical/artifacts/caricatures/
An amusing site with 19th century cartoons, many of them about health and medicine.

http://www.whonamedit.com/
A detailed encyclopaedia of medical people.

http://americanhistory.si.edu/polio/
The Smithsonian's National Museum of American History site on polio, covering American epidemics, how polio changed the U.S., the virus and the vaccine, and polio today.

http://www.cwru.edu/artsci/dittrick/site2/
Dittrick Medical History Center homepage with online exhibits. Under related sites, there is a link to history of medicine resources, with a listing of medical museums, archives and libraries in the U.S.

http://medhist.ac.uk:80/index.html
Homepage of MedHist, gateway to Internet resources for the History of Medicine.

Places to visit

Mutter Museum, College of Physicians, Philadelphia, PA
One of the oldest medical museums in the U.S.
www.collphyphil.org/muttpg1.shtml

Museum of Science, Boston, MA
On the cutting edge of science education, innovative, interactive exhibits range from bugs, and supernovas to the medical x-ray and contemporary medical imaging techniques
www.mos.org

Bakken Library and Museum, Minneapolis, MN
Exhibits and collections related to the history of electricity and magnetism in medicine and the life sciences.
www.thebakken.org

John P. McGovern Museum of Health & Medical Science, Houston, TX
Features larger than life anatomical models and interactive exhibits.
www.mhms.org

Index

American Medical Association 47, 49
anaesthetics 41
anatomy 10-11
Anatomy Act (1832) 10
anthrax 21, 26
antiseptic surgery 42-43
aseptic surgery 43

Barton, Clara 35
BCG 27
Beaumont, William 15
Bedlam Asylum 54
Behring, Emil 27
Bernard, Claude 13
Billroth, Theodor 42
Blackwell, Elizabeth 48-49
British Medical Association 47
Broussais, Francois 13
Burke and Hare 10

Calmette and Guerin 27
cancer 17, 45
cell theory 16
Chadwick, Edwin 33
Chamberland, Charles 27
chemotherapy 45
Chicago Sanitary and Ship canal 37
chiropractor 52
chloroform 41
cholera 6-7, 21, 27
Crimean War 34
Curie, Marie and Pierre 45

Darwin, Charles 8
diptheria 27
Dix, Dorothea 54
doctors 4, 5, 46-47, 50-51
Dunant, Henri 35

Ehrlich, Paul 44-45
electrocardiograph 15
ether 41
eugenics 9, 55

Flexner report 47, 49
Four Humors 20, 44
Frankenstein 11

Gall, Franz Josef 55
Galton, Francis 8
Garrett, Elizabeth 48-49
germ theory 22-23

Gorgas, William Crawford 29
Graham, Sylvester 53
Gray's Anatomy (1858) 11

homeopathy 52
hormones 14
humoral pathology 17, 10
hydropathy 52
hygienists 32-35

immunology 26-27

Jenner, Edward 18-19
Jex-Blake, Sophia 48-49

Kellogg, Will Keith 53
Kitasato, Shibasaburo 25, 27
Koch, Robert 9, 22, 24, 25, 27
Kocher, Theodor 43
kymograph 15

Laennec, Rene 12
Lancet, The 47
Lister, Joseph 42-43
Lister, Joseph Jackson 11, 16
Long, William Crawford 41
Louis, Pierre 13, 44

"magic bullets" 44-45
Manson, Patrick 28
Medical Repository, The 47
Mendel, Gregor 8
mental health 54-55
Metchnikoff, Elie 26
miasma 20-21
microscope 11, 16
Modern Physician, The 50-51

Nightingale, Florence 34-35
Nitrous Oxide (laughing gas) 41

osteopath 52

Panama Canal 29
Pasteur, Louis 9, 19, 22-23, 25, 26
pasteurization 23
Pavlov, Ivan 14
Pemberton, John Stith 57
phrenology 55

physiology 13-16
plague (bubonic) 25, 27
public health 30-37
Purkinje, Jan 13

quacks 52-53

rabies 26
radium 45
Red Cross 35
reductionism 14
Ruge, Carl 39
Rush, Benjamin 5, 32, 54

salvarsan 606 45
sanatoria 45
Sequah 53
Shattuck, Lemuel 33
Simpson, James 41
Sims, James Marion 38
smallpox 18-19
Snow, John 21, 41
Spanish flu 44
Starling and Bayliss 14
stethoscope 12
surgery 38-43

tropical medicine 28-29
tuberculosis 4, 7
Typhoid Mary 58-59

variolation 18
Villerme, Louis 32
Virchow, Rudolf 17, 33
vitamins 15

Warren, John Collins 41
Welch, William Henry 13, 25
Wendell Holmes, Oliver 5, 41, 42
women doctors 48-49
Wright, Almroth 27

X-rays 15
yellow fever 4, 29
Yersin, Alexandre 25

DATE DUE